NEON FUSION

Painting Radiant Art with Acrylic
Brilliance

Chelsea Alex

Table of Contents

CHAPTER ONE

INTRODUCTION

Neon acrylic paint is an undeniable option if you really want to give your white gesso painting a neon-revived appearance and add more interest. Neon inks can likewise be immediately applied with shower paint or electronic printing, making a dazzling difference. For added strength, utilize five star acrylic paints that are guarded to tangling and hurt from barometrical circumstances or standard mileage. Acrylic diamonds are great gifts for any occasion, whether you're looking for something truly unique for yourself or someone special. All things considered, prior to getting an insistence, thoroughly check it out. Contingent upon your necessities, there might be better choices accessible. An acrylic painting can be on an unbelievably essential level changed with the help of white gesso and acrylic paint. Using sprinkle paint and mechanized printing, you can give your jewel a splash of color. An acrylic painting with a neon feel is perfect for making a shocking mix of blends in any room. You can create a truly charming masterpiece that stands out from the obstruction by utilizing various tones and designs. Neon acrylic paint gives your white gesso painting a neon-pushed look and is great for stirring it up. Along these lines, neon inks can be bought related to modernized printing or shower paint to create a really remarkable outcome in a more limited measure of time. For more power, use acrylic paints with a five-star rating that discussion with obscuration and tricky from cools or regular mileage. Whether you're looking for something particularly staggering for yourself or someone else in your life, imaginative acrylic signs make remarkable gifts for any occasion. Second acrylic pearls are available online at make supply stores; Moreover, before making a purchase, check the guarantee because there may be better options available depending on your needs.

How should acrylic be impacted by neon paint?

White gesso and acrylic paint can be used to alter an acrylic painting. Neon inks can be applied to your suit with shower paint or electronic printing to add tone. An acrylic painting with a neon impact can leave a charming scratching of blending in any room. By using various tones and systems, you can make a truly gigantic jewel that stands confined from the resistance. Cover your framework with a layer of white gesso going before utilizing acrylic paint. Over the gesso, paint neon acrylic in different examples utilizing light and vaporous brushstrokes to make a spellbinding difference. Before applying any final nuances or subtleties, allow the paint to dry completely. Utilize white gesso and acrylic paint to make different implications for different pieces of your space for never-endingly out more energy. Have a go at painting neon acrylic on a light foundation to get a really massive turn that will stay aware of carefulness to even the Neon expressive graph. Shower paint or express level printing can solidify neon inks to have a dumbfounding effect. Any reputable tool shop carries neon inks. To accomplish the neon impact, different shades of ink are applied to a substrate that gives the impression of being portrayal paper, material, or wood. You'll require a few focal supplies like acrylic paint, dull light LEDs and cerebrum blowing lights for the gig. To get everything going, blend white acrylic paint with the right neon tone until you get the right shade. Apply a layer of clear sealant to reestablish the quality and guarantee fulfillment when you are satisfied with the outcome. Acrylic paint can be used to have a neon-like effect in a piece by establishing white and dull to make shades of sensitive. Then, utilizing sensitive brushes or puddles of blend, spread the neon-shrouded away pours over the material. Allow the material to completely dry before adding any final contacts, such as finished parts or shine, for a more authentic appearance. With its short neon attitude, permit it an amazing chance to add extraordinarily dull perspectives and lights to your creative endeavors.

What Impacts Ought to Paint Neon Have on Acrylic?

With respect to giving your white gesso painting a neon-reestablished look and adding an additional pop of assortment, neon acrylic paint is a sure decision. You can correspondingly add neon inks with shower paint or modernized printing to have a more temperamental impact essentially speedier. Use solid acrylic paints that are immune to blurring and hurt from the environment or standard use for more power. Acrylic pieces make phenomenal gifts for any event, whether you're searching for something strikingly goliath for yourself or a mate or relative. Second acrylic signs are open online at make supply stores; in any case, preceding making a purchase, endeavor to look at the interest first since there may be better decisions open depending upon what you're looking for.

How might Paint Neon maybe essentially influence Acrylic?

An acrylic painting can be changed with white gesso and acrylic paint. To make your game arrangement stick out, you can use modernized printing or neon inks with shower paint. Any room can be given a dazzling impression of intermixing by hanging an acrylic painting in neon tones. By joining different tones and plan, you can make a truly phenomenal piece of craftsmanship that will stand bound from the rest.

MAKE GAME ARRANGEMENTS USING WHITE GESSO AND ACRYLIC PAINT

To begin, apply a layer of white gesso. Paint neon acrylic over the gesso on a variety of models with light, wavy brushstrokes to create a striking contrast. Allow the paint to completely dry before adding any final nuances or subtleties. With white gesso and acrylic paint, look at different streets to comprehend for different area of your space for extra motivation.

Have a go at painting neon acrylic on a dull surface before all else for a truly captivating look that will advance forward through even among Neon complex plans. Use Neon Inks connected with Modernized Printing or Shower Paint Neon inks are speedily open at all striking specialty stores. They can be used with clear level printing or shower paint to have a stunning neon effect. The neon influence is given by applying various shades of ink to a substrate, similar to paper, material, or wood tending to. The occasion requires acrylic paint, LEDs for faint lighting, and unimaginable lights. To get everything rolling, join the fitting neon tone with white acrylic paint until the ideal shade is accomplished. Right when you are happy with the outcome, apply a layer of clear sealant to shield the satisfaction and add additional greatness.

CHAPTER TWO

CREATE AN ACRYLIC PAINTING WITH A NEON EFFECT

To achieve a neon-like effect with acrylic paint, first lay out a sheet of white and blend it together to create shades of gray. Then, coordinate appearances of neon tones to the material utilizing put brushes or puddles of plan down. Grant the material to thoroughly dry going before adding any last contacts, as finished parts or sparkle, to other than speak with validness. As exhibited by a neon point of view, quickly endeavor to coordinate magnificently molded scenes and lights into your incomprehensible vision. Stain your completed work on the grounds that staggering groupings will crumble after some time. How could it be that it may be the case that reality may ultimately demonstrate the way that you could Make Acrylic Paint Look Neon? Neon cover powder and acrylic paint can be utilized together to have a neon impact. Painting frameworks can be used to achieve the best appearance, and Stir it Up Powder can be used to create the specific gathering you need. For an amazing neon influence, join various shades of neon in an imaginative way. Obviously acrylic appearances are reasonable for accomplishing this engaged appearance; as per a general perspective, utilize what's happening.

How is it that it could be that acrylic could paint making such a tremendous difference?

Paint the most raised spot of your wick with white acrylic paint. Brush the paint around the wick with a light hand and mix it into unpleasant umber. Around the fire, leave a little, disturbing game plan of umber; this will give the impression that manual labor is lighting the interior. Right when you're content with your magnificence influence, dispose of any excess white paint using a q-tip or piece of paper towel hosed in turpentine oil; Keep away from over-cleaning.

THE BEST WAY TO MAKE NEON PURPLE WITH ACRYLIC PAINT

The central thing to do while using acrylic paint to make neon purple is to combine white and dull as one until you get a light purple. Then, for a truly unstable sound, add blue and yellow. You should join two or three explicit shades of acrylic paint until you track down the best shade to make a neon purple utilizing acrylic paint. You'll correspondingly have to endeavor to use good paint so that it's thick and drenched, and endeavor to blend it an unquestionably expanded time interval going before permitting it to totally dry.

Watchfully apply your Neon Purple material after everything has dried.

Might you at whatever point make neon with key tones?

Without a doubt, you can make neon with critical tones using various supplies. Little, stacked gas and light chambers are utilized to move neon. At the point when lit, the bulbs transmit a staggering shimmer that is ordinarily utilized for promoting and signage. To Make Neon Paint, You'll Need Phenomenal Fluorescent Tones You'll require remarkable fluorescent tones that are coordinated as such to make neon paint. These paints are the more reliably and taken out a chance to dry than standard paint, so show obstruction while working with them. It won't attempt to blend different boss tones; they will basically obliterate mud. Test each new neon paint completely prior to putting it on your wall or another surface. Expecting you see that the assortment is irrationally silly or doesn't look right, start with a more harmed structure right away.

Neon Paints Are More really than Ordinary Paint

Neon paints are on a particularly crucial level more perseveringly than normal paints and can expect up to two hours to absolutely dry.

1. This prescribes that you should allow palatable time for the area you're painting to completely dry going before technique - overall around your pearl could come relaxed in minutes. Earnestly take the necessary steps not to Endeavor to Blend Neon Tones with Other Head Groupings Blending neon tones with other huge tones will dependably make a gigantic mix of shades that won't look wonderful on any surface. Keep using bright fluorescents because, all things considered, they will display their true substance much better.

2. To conclude, always remember: Neon paint should be quieted start with nothing in any way shape or form and evaluate until you track down the best shade for

your endeavor. Always Test a Clear Total of New Paint Before beginning any project, including neon paint, consistently test a clear total on a piece of paper or another non-delicate object before generously applying it to your planned irrelevant target. If something turns out savagely (i.e., Expecting the paint gets foaming and giving rolling unpleasant exhaust, you'll see rapidly what should be fixed rather than with nothing to do endeavoring to fix something genuinely not broken.

Might You at whatever point whenever Make Standard Acrylic Paint Shimmer In lack of clarity?

Unquestionably, you can. All you truly need is a light source and some brilliance without definition paint. Apply the paint to your material or other surface by blending it in with water until it has a smooth consistency. Place the article in direct light for about an hour after it has dried to ensure that the paint has totally acted. You can make standard acrylic paint look dull by utilizing a remarkable fluorescent paint. This kind of paint is clear and will allow you to see the obscure assortment when painted under an UV light. Sparkle in fogginess paints are open all that considered specialty stores, or you can make your own using some normal family embellishments.

How Could You Make Shimmer In haziness Paint?

To make a splendor in dimness paint, you ought to join as one 1:2 powders to paint. You can charge your paint by introducing it to light or sunlight. Apply your mix to a surface where it has been charged and grant it to thoroughly dry before it becomes faint. This reasonable DIY errand will allow you to participate in your adequately magnificent spaces for a colossal time frame range.

What tone attracts neon purple?

Neon purple is made of a blend of different tones. The more senseless each tone is, the genuinely astounding the neon purple will be. Use your bluest red and reddest blue to create amazing neon purple. To sum up, neon paint is a shocking structure for accomplishing an acrylic neon impact. Neon Purple Lighting can help you with finishing up which tones to use for your assignment. You can make any tone or model you want by layering different Neon paints together. When painting, make sure to follow all safety precautions because neon paint can be very dangerous if applied improperly.

CHAPTER THREE

CONTEMPLATIONS FOR NEON PAINTING

Tips and Deludes for a Brilliant and Serious Gem painting is a remarkable and fun method for flaunting your innovative side. This kind of painting concretes using incredible groupings to make a striking and eye-getting ideal masterpiece. Even though it may give the impression that you are constantly sabotaging, with a little practice, you can create fantastic neon connections that will stun your loved ones. In this article, we will answer several standard referencing concerning neon painting, as well as give two or three essential hints to help you with getting everything moving. Overall, what do you anticipate? Get some paint and start making.

How precisely does neon painting work and what precisely is it?

Neon painting is a type of light workmanship that makes a precariousness of focusing light by utilizing fluorescent or great paint. The effect is achieved by applying the paint to a dull surface, which makes the neon tones appear to "pop" against the shadowiness. There are two techniques for accomplishing neon painting: both a prompt and indirect application. At the point when paint is applied in a wicked way, it is first applied to a white surface prior to continuing on toward a dull surface. Direct application happens when the paint is applied obviously to the dull surface. The impact you want to have and your own tendencies will determine which strategy you use. Direct application may be staggering expecting you stay aware of that your neon creative appearances should look more three-layered. The indirect application may be the best methodology in the event that you need a more unobtrusive impact. Overlooking which procedure you use, there are a few enormous things while painting with neon tones. Working in a room with great ventilation is particularly significant in light of the fact that paint exhaust can be upsetting. Basically, gloves and careful dress ought to be worn considering the way that the paint can be extremely muddled. Finally, make sure you have plenty of time set aside for your project because neon extraordinary sights can take a few hours or even days to complete. Expecting that you're new to painting with neon tones, these plans will start you off. Any room can be illuminated in a senseless and unique manner with neon craftsmanship. In any case, knowing the nuts and bolts of neon painting is crucial before you start.

Coming up next are several pointers for newbie's:

1. Select your tones circumspectly at first. The most captivating groupings will be the

brilliant ones, yet you should likewise examine the general tone of your craftsmanship. For example, on the off chance that you're fanning out a painting, you ought to incorporate lighter tones for a more delicate impact.

2. Then, think about your subject. Both illustrative and keep plans can be made with neon works of art. To paint, have a go at endeavoring various things with different shapes and models. Light and shadow can similarly be used to make interest and importance.

3. Make a pass at a novel, new thing to wrap things up. Notwithstanding the way that neon paints can be dangerous to work with, this is basic for the phenomenal

times. Take the necessary steps not to hold some place close to any means to endeavor different things with new philosophies and game-plan mixes. The outcomes that could happen are incomprehensible. In the event that you don't have any idea where to begin, attempt one of the thoughts for neon painting underneath.

A nearby sprout: This is astonishing heading for beginners since it is really clear and doesn't need ludicrous detail. Use conveying energies, and feel free to attempt new things!

A cityscape around night: This is clever if you want to have a really exciting effect. Utilizing both stunning and faint tones is basic for conveying a sensation of significance.

A portrayal of a pal or relative: You can really change your imaginative creation by doing this. Fundamentally, you ought to attempt to utilize eye-getting assortments that will stand apart from the standard base.

A hypothetical blueprint: This is a good idea for people who need to endeavor various things with different mixes and shapes. Just let your creative energies stream and see what you can plan! Your neon show-stoppers are related with being striking and creative, so go ahead and endeavor new things with them!

EXTRA MADE PROCEDURES FOR PAINTING NEON

In the wake of dominating the basics, you can begin investigating extra made methods for painting neon. A few intends to kick you off are as per the following:

• Neon Split-Fundamental Tones is a framework that uses two blends that are connecting each other on the assortment wheel, close by a third blend that is an opposite thing to those two tones. Hence, there is a conceivably enormous difference impact.

• Neon Blend Ending, joins using isolating assortments to make numerical shapes and models. This can be used to make interesting ideal experiences or just over add an extra soul to your work of art.

• One of the most unimaginably completely seen advanced structures is blending. Experts are able to create an astounding number of brand-new tones and shades by carefully combining various paint shades.

• Layering is a technique that can be utilized to foster little groupings or to make importance and perspective. One way to layer paint on your surface is to apply a number of small layers of different colors and patterns.

• The ombré influence, which makes an inclination by using various shades of paint, Start by painting the entire light box in a dull assortment for an ombré influence. Then, at that point, working beginning from the top, dependably add lighter shades of paint until you show up at the best effect.

• Despite what the basic neon painting structure, there are in addition different ways to deal with supervising having different surfaces and effects. One run of the mill methodology is to use a completed brush or wipe to apply the paint. This might deliver a spotted outcome that mirrors the brilliance of the night sky's stars. Another procedure for adding surface is to mix the paint in with sand or rock. A coarser surface will result from this, which can be used to enhance a vast, level surface.

• With everything taken into account, several specialists like to work on their pearls with sparkle or different embellishments. It is dependably used to upgrade shadows and parts or, all the something else overall, to add a spot of appeal. First, combine shine and clear paint to create a glittery paste with a neon shimmer. Then, using a little brush, apply the marvel paste to the district of your piece that you wish to organize. For best results, use a feeble light to see your relationship while you work, as this will help you with seeing where the magnificence is generally speaking undeniable. When you're done, allow the paint to completely dry before adding any more colors or accents. In manifestations, neon light can be utilized to deliver various results. The extraordinary thought of neon light can outfit your show-stoppers with an impression of secret or dynamic quality. You can make genuinely inventive neon creates in the event that you know how to set up the force of light. It is key for break down the general tone of your synthesis while working with neon light. For example, assuming you really need to make energy of energy, you could use more surprising plans and more insane light. Naturally, if you want a truly calming effect, you could choose collections with less force and lighting. Your speculations can benefit from neon light in a variety of ways. A solitary open door is to incorporate it as foundation lighting by sparkling it through direct materials like glass or plastic. This will have a sparkling effect that can give your creation more weight and perspective. Another decision is to paint clearly with a neon light. This ought to be conceivable by using fluorescent paint or by putting neon tubes behind your material. Endeavor various frameworks to see which one suits you and your strategy for overseeing painting the best. You can create neon masterpieces that are packed with life and energy by making use of light's force.

Utilize the light to give your work more weight and force, and let your innovative soul radiate through. Neon masterpieces are a kind of light creation that usages mind blowing, shining tones to convey an eye getting influence. Tolerating that gotten along excellently, neon craftsmanship can make it lights-out time for you. Coming up next are a couple of strategies for making your own splendid neon pearls:

Pick the right tones: Concerning neon materials, more heavenly is reliably better. Dynamic pinks, greens, and blues will convey the most striking outcome.

Use a black light: Under common light, neon paints are dim, yet when acquainted with black light, they shimmer extraordinarily. Endeavor to set up your black light before you start painting.

Utilize shadows to increase depth: Your masterpiece may gain significance and perspective from shadows. Conceals that are more dull will seem to vanish from view, while lighter shades will seem to jump off the page.

Permit the paint to air dry: Neon paint dries quickly, so you'll need to work fast. Anyway, you ought to hang on for each layer of paint to dry going before adding another top completely. Your magnum opus could seem spread out or more obscure in certain spots.

Where might you at some point get thoughts for your next neon painting experience?

There are different wellsprings of motivation on the planet, whether you're a created informed power or basically starting and attempting to figure things out bound. The next thing is just beginning to show what's underneath, but it can give experts some unique ideas to think about before starting another pearl project!

Nature: Have a go at checking out at nature first. The world is loaded up with enthusiastic gatherings and models, making it a stunning wellspring of neon pieces' motivation. Neon synthesis, for example, could be captivated by a splendidly lit sunset or a completely dark woodland. Then again, you could focus in on extra tangled nuances like fledglings or birds.

Workmanship history: Try looking through the history of craftsmanship if you're not feeling particularly inspired. An immense heap of the managers surveyed unbelievable mixes for their work, making them a phenomenal wellspring of inspiration for neon materials. With its striking tones, neon would look amazing in paintings like "Mind blowing Night" by Vincent van Gogh and "Water Lilies" by Claude Monet, for instance. Obviously, you could zero in on dumbfounding state of the art experts who use stunning mixes in their work.

Web-based presentations include: In case you do an expedient request on the web, neon paint can be found on various gems. If you don't know near anything about where to start, research a piece of your vitally master's complaints or online shows for inspiration.

Books and magazines: There are a great deal of books and magazines focused in on craftsmanship and plan, tremendous extents of which mix neon paint on their pages. Consider a couple of your top choices for assessments and charm on the most able technique to coordinate this kind of paint into your work.

Close by craftsmanship supply stores: Neon paints are overall open at a get-together of craftsmanship supply stores. Seeing how different blueprints seem when applied to paper or material can be fun here. Besides, many stores offer classes on painting with neon tones, permitting you the potential chance to practice under the bearing of a cultivated teacher.

Viewpoint on the nearby city: Cityscapes can be given more life and interest by neon lights. Take a walk around your area or visit a nearby city and see how neon is used without genuinely attempting to cover spaces. The utilization

of neon to make affiliations and plans
could act for instance.

THE END

www.ingramcontent.com/pod-product-compliance
Lightning Source LLC
Chambersburg PA
CBHW071015290526
45795CB00005B/1806